THIS WALKER BOOK BELONGS TO:

For Joe Nethercott K.W.
For Freddy P.M.
– and with thanks to David Macdonald of the
Department of Zoology, Oxford, for his help and advice

Red foxes are found in Europe, Asia, northern Africa and North America. They
are very adaptable and will live almost anywhere – in woods, by the sea or in towns.
To see a fox by day is quite unusual: foxes are much more active at night.

First published 1994 by Walker Books Ltd, 87 Vauxhall Walk, London SE11 5HJ

This edition published 1996

2 4 6 8 10 9 7 5 3 1

Text © 1994 Karen Wallace, illustrations © 1994 Peter Melnyczuk

This book has been typeset in Plantin Light. Printed in Hong Kong

British Library Cataloguing in Publication Data

A catalogue record for this book is available from the British Library.

ISBN 0-7445-4361-4

Red Fox

Written by Karen Wallace
Illustrated by Peter Melnyczuk

WALKER BOOKS
AND SUBSIDIARIES
LONDON • BOSTON • SYDNEY

Red fox is
in the meadow.
His coat is bright
like a flame.

He zigzags
through the grass.
His tail floats behind him
like a banner.

*The tip of a fox's tail is called a tag.
It is often white.*

In winter, a fox's fur is thicker.

9

Red fox is hungry.
His black nose
skims along the ground,
searching for a mouse.

When a fox trots, he puts his back left foot in the prints
of his front right foot, and his back right foot in the prints
of his front left foot, leaving a straight line of prints behind him.

10

Suddenly he pounces!

Red fox traps
a mouse in his paws
and holds it tight
against the grass.

Foxes also eat rabbits, insects,
worms, fruit and birds.

His wild eyes flick
from side to side.
He lifts his nose
and sniffs the air.
He waits until
he's sure he is alone.

All wild animals need to feel safe
when they're eating.
Another animal could attack them
or try to steal their food.

Then he carries the mouse
into the long grass
and eats it
in two mouthfuls.

Half hidden
in the roots of a tree
three cubs are
watching him.

Fox cubs are born in early March.
They stay in their den until
they are four weeks old.

A male fox is called a dog fox.
A female is called a vixen.

Their eyes are shiny.
Their faces are stubby.
One of them chews
an earthworm.
They are too young
to hunt in the meadow.

When the cubs are small, the dog fox
and the vixen bring food to the den.
As they grow older, they learn
to fend for themselves.

20

The sun is hot.
Red fox yawns
and licks his lips.
He stretches his neck
and turns like a dog
to flatten the grass.

When you see a flattened patch of grass in a field, it may be a sign that foxes have been lying or playing there.

Above him
a branch cracks
and crashes
to the ground.
Red fox jumps.

A fox's ears are very sensitive.
They can hear the rustle of a beetle
a metre or more away.

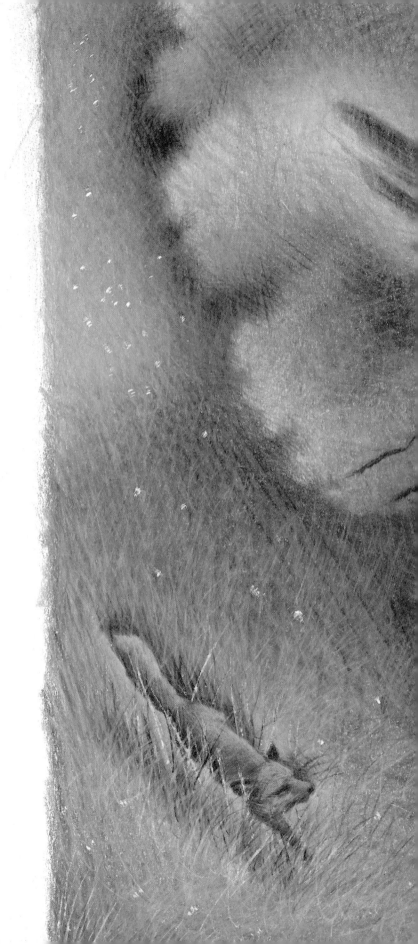

24

His body stiffens.
He bunches the
muscles in his legs.
He barks to the cubs
to hide in the den.

*A fox's warning bark is short
and gruff, like the bark of a dog.*

Then he runs
as fast as he can
where no one
will find him.

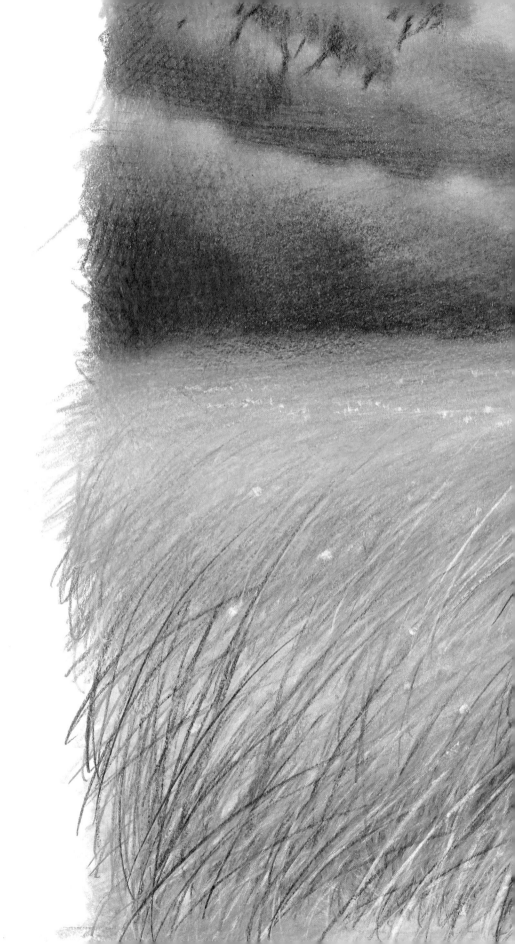

Look up the pages to find
out about all these fox things.
Don't forget to look at both kinds
of words: this kind and *this kind*.

MORE WALKER PAPERBACKS
For You to Enjoy

"These books fulfil all the requirements of a factual picture book,
but also supply that imaginative element." *The Independent on Sunday*

"Beautifully illustrated books, written with style and humour."
The Times Educational Supplement

I LOVE GUINEA-PIGS
by Dick King-Smith/Anita Jeram
0-7445-4725-3   £4.99

ALL PIGS ARE BEAUTIFUL
by Dick King-Smith/Anita Jeram
0-7445-3635-9   £4.99

RED FOX
by Karen Wallace/Peter Melnyczuk
0-7445-4361-4   £4.99

TOWN PARROT
by Penelope Bennett/Sue Heap
0-7445-4727-X   £4.99

I LIKE MONKEYS BECAUSE...
by Peter Hansard/Patricia Casey
0-7445-3646-4   £4.99

THINK OF AN EEL
by Karen Wallace/Mike Bostock
(Winner of the Times Educational Supplement's Junior Information
Book Award and the Kurt Maschler Award)
0-7445-3639-1   £4.99

CATERPILLAR CATERPILLAR
by Vivian French/Charlotte Voake
Shortlisted for the Kurt Maschler Award
0-7445-3636-7   £4.99

A FIELD FULL OF HORSES
by Peter Hansard/Kenneth Lilly
0-7445-3645-6   £4.99

Walker Paperbacks are available from most booksellers, or by post from B.B.C.S., P.O. Box 941, Hull, North Humberside HU1 3YQ

24 hour telephone credit card line 01482 224626

To order, send: Title, author, ISBN number and price for each book ordered, your full name and address,
cheque or postal order payable to BBCS for the total amount and allow the following for postage and packing:
UK and BFPO: £1.00 for the first book, and 50p for each additional book to a maximum of £3.50.
Overseas and Eire: £2.00 for the first book, £1.00 for the second and 50p for each additional book.

Prices and availability are subject to change without notice.